D1535718

Praise for *Drawn from the Hea...*

Leave it to Lisa Bogart to come up with a project that soothes and stimulates the creative heart.

Debbie Macomber, #1 *New York Times* best-selling author

Studies have shown that coloring relaxes us and puts us in a meditative spot. Combine coloring with devotionals and you not only have a bright idea, but a wonderful way to ponder and deepen our relationship with God while we color. *Drawn from the Heart* is a wonderful coloring book devotional that will feed your creativity while inspiring your heart and mind.

Georgia Shaffer, author of *Avoiding the 12 Relationship Mistakes Women Make*, Christian life coach, and PA licensed psychologist

As a Christian counselor and coach, I always knew how therapeutic art could be, but I never actually experienced it until recently when I picked up my pens and paints and started to draw and paint. Lisa's book, *Drawn from the Heart*, not only provides great thoughts to ponder, but she also creates pages for you to color. Try it. It's not only fun and releases stress, it actually helps you remember what you just read.

Leslie Vernick, licensed counselor, relationship coach, and author of 7 books, including *The Emotionally Destructive Relationship* and *The Emotionally Destructive Marriage*

Add crayons and colored pencils to your tools of praise! If Lisa Bogart had just written a book of meditations on quotes from Charles Schulz, Madeleine L'Engle, and reflections on verses of scripture and classic hymns, her musings would be more than enough to commend her joyous new book, *Drawn From the Heart*. But Lisa goes where no devotional book has gone before. She also created a full page of art as a companion to each entry. Lisa's art is delightfully refreshing, surprising in its variety, and explosive in its exuberance. So inspiring!

C. McNair Wilson, author/speaker *HATCH!: Brainstorming Secrets of A Theme Park Designer*

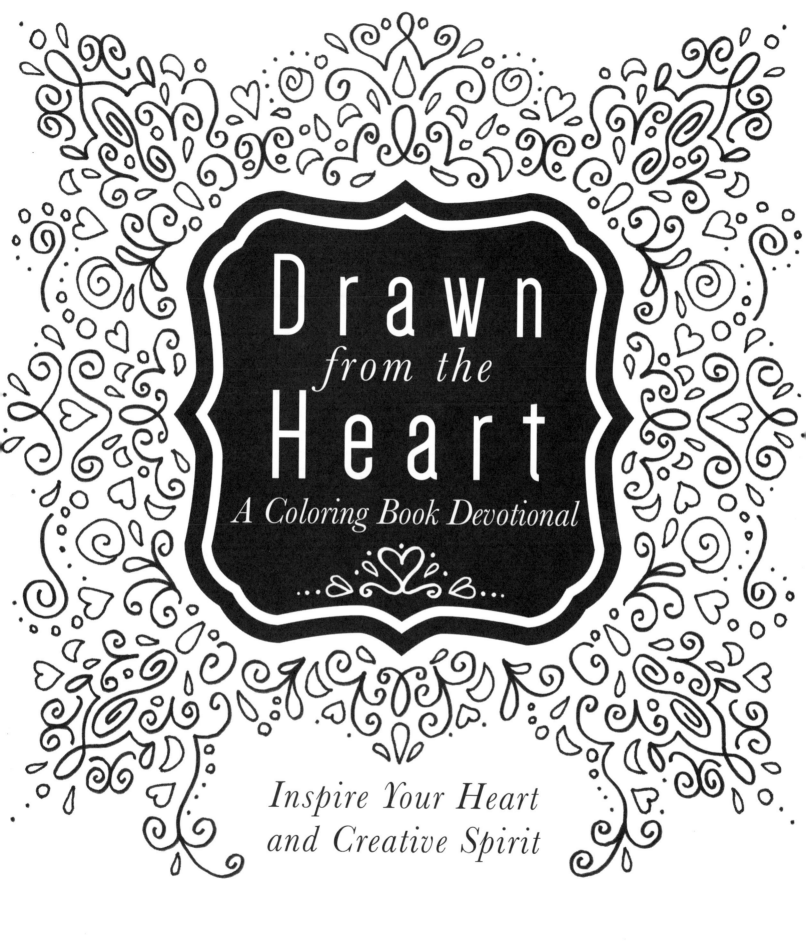

Drawn
from the
Heart
A Coloring Book Devotional

*Inspire Your Heart
and Creative Spirit*

LISA BOGART

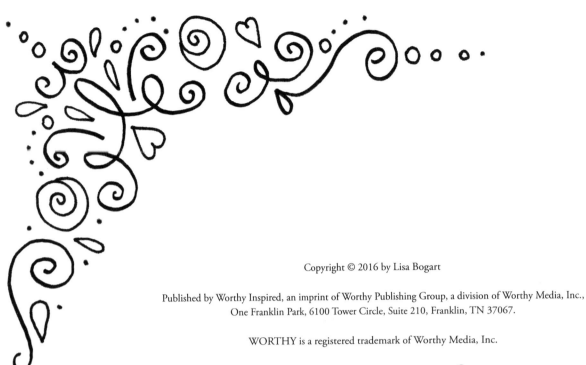

Published by Worthy Inspired, an imprint of Worthy Publishing Group, a division of Worthy Media, Inc.,
One Franklin Park, 6100 Tower Circle, Suite 210, Franklin, TN 37067.

WORTHY is a registered trademark of Worthy Media, Inc.

HELPING PEOPLE EXPERIENCE THE HEART OF GOD

Library of Congress Control Number: 2015959357

ISBN: 978-1-61795-733-8

For foreign and subsidiary rights, contact rights@worthypublishing.com.

Cover Design: Jeff Jansen / Aesthetic Soup
Cover and Interior Illustrations: Lisa Bogart

Printed in the United States of America

16 17 18 19 20 21 RRD 11 10 9 8 7 6 5 4 3 2 1

Contents

Introduction: What Is This? — 1

1. Praise Him with Every Good Gift — 2
2. Sweet Words — 4
3. Laugh-Out-Loud Funny! — 6
4. Little Gift, Big Deal — 8
5. Think On This — 10
6. Noticing the Details — 12
7. Stand Up — 14
8. Passion — 16
9. People Watching — 18
10. Hundreds, Thousands, Millions — 20
11. Sharing the Harvest — 22
12. Look at It This Way . . . — 26
13. Yours the Glory — 28
14. Surprised by Sparkles — 30
15. I Got This — 32
16. Sunny Mail — 34
17. Seize the Moment — 36
18. Rubbing It In — 38
19. Surrounded — 40
20. Little Influence — 42
21. Counting My Blessings — 44
22. It Is Well with My Soul — 46
23. Stop. — 48
24. He Is Risen Indeed! — 50
25. Anchored — 52
26. I Will Listen — 54
27. Wandering Off — 58
28. Shared Beauty — 60
29. Be My Guest — 62
30. Star Gazing — 64
31. Traveler Assistance — 66
32. Great Expectations — 68
33. Foundations — 70
34. Teamwork — 72
35. With Eyes of Love — 74
36. Forgiveness — 76
37. A Good Parting — 78
38. A Tune of Trust — 80
39. Tiny Bubbles — 82
40. Vacation Bible School — 84

Acknowledgments — 88

What is This?

A devotional you color? A drawing you read?

This unique book is the happy combination of both: a collection of devotions to engage your mind and a gallery of drawings to feed your

Creativity

I have doodled for as long as I can remember. I love putting pencil to paper, and I especially love drawing letter forms. Even in this digital age, I pull out my paper and markers and doodle a few lines. I get lost in the squiggles and soon have made pages of drawings.

And I am always on the lookout for devotional moments. Those fleeting times I can connect the dots to find a little lesson or glimpse seeing God move in my world. I treasure those flights of inspiration—they feed my writing, and they give me points to ponder when I draw.

Now it is my pleasure to share these with you. I hope you will grab some crayons, find some colored pencils or buy some brand new markers and take the plunge into a little creative time. Read a devotion and then have fun coloring the drawing. Let your mind wander as you work; you will have time for the words to really sink in. And don't stop with my lines; add some embellishments. Make this book your own!

ENJOY!

Lisa

Praise Him with Every Good Gift

Praise God, from Whom all blessings flow;
Praise Him, all creatures here below;
Praise Him above, ye heavenly host;
Praise Father, Son, and Holy Ghost.

Thomas Ken

Hallelujah! Praise God any way you want! You could be in a choir of hundreds or alone in your kitchen. You could be singing rock music or chanting. Hymns could be played on a magnificent pipe organ or contemporary tunes with an electronic accompaniment. Music of every stripe and variety can fill a place of worship. If it's sung to God, about God, and for God, it's music to God's ear.

But why stop there? We have so many options beyond our voices. Dance. Run. Paint. Garden. Swim. Sculpt. Knit. Drive. Whistle. Any way you can express yourself is a way to praise to God. We are not locked into a formula for giving God our praise. Of course, having a set form helps us put our thoughts and praise into a neat package we can give to God, but it's not essential. We are free to rejoice over Him any way our hearts move.

Thomas Ken wrote this hymn, *Awake My Soul and with the Sun,* in the 1600s, a time when the established church thought only the words of scripture could be sung in church. Some even thought it was blasphemous to write new lyrics for church music. It's rather ironic that a song never meant to be sung in church is used to conclude many services today. Happily we can express ourselves more freely in this century. But how comforting to have Ken's words to conclude a church service and send us on our way rejoicing.

Service is a great way to offer praise to God. My Catholic upbringing was filled with the phrase, "Offer it up." I really had no idea what that meant till I was much older and I realized I can offer my service as praise to God. The time I spend in service can be a time of prayer and thanksgiving. Time I spend cleaning or setting up chairs or washing or cooking can be time I concentrate on why I am serving in the first place. I can use my work to praise God.

And we can use our pleasure to praise God too. Coloring is a lovely way to slow down, relax your mind, and let your spirit turn to praise. I encourage you to smile as you select your colors, to feel content as you make your marks, and to find joy in your creating. This time is yours to offer praise to God.

I praise You with my voice, Father.
And I'm praising You with my time and talent and creativity.
Thank You for all the ways I can express my joy in You.

Amen

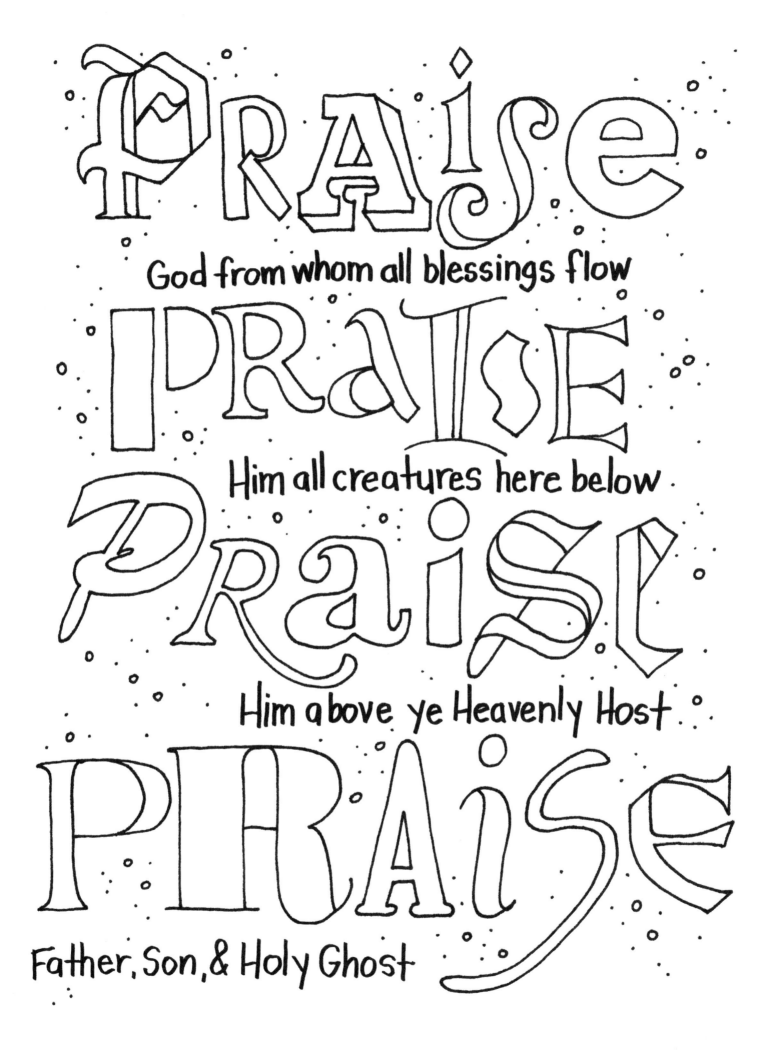

Praise God from whom all blessings flow
Praise Him all creatures here below
Praise Him above ye Heavenly Host
Praise Father, Son, & Holy Ghost

Sweet Words

Gracious words are a honeycomb,
sweet to the soul and healing to the bones.
Proverbs 16:24

It's fun when my circles of friends intersect. One of the questions they always ask each other is, "So, how do you know Lisa?" The defining factor is often an activity we share: bell choir, knit group, writing class, church buddy. Every once in a while, someone will describe me in terms of an act of kindness. That warms my heart but surprises me at the same time. I have often forgotten the very thing they remember so vividly.

I introduced my work friend Christine to my knit friend Stephanie. "This is my friend the Doctor!" I told Stephanie. Christine laughed. I explained, "Christine just got her PhD! We work in the knit shop together. Everyone in the shop is so proud of her. We like to introduce her as Dr., Dr. Knit! Actually she earned a doctorate in geology and teaches at a college. And she really does have knit doctor skills as well."

Christine smiled and filled in her side of the story. "Last January when all of us from the knit shop had our holiday team dinner I was stressing out about my PhD dissertation. It was going to be a long haul to May when I had to give my defense. I almost broke down when the gals started peppering me with questions and trying to give me advice. I couldn't deal with it. I asked them to stop. I would handle it on my own, thank you very much. My next shift in the shop I found a note in my box. Lisa wrote to give me some encouragement."

Huh? I didn't even remember writing her a note. It's just something I do. I saw a friend hurting and figured she could use a good word of support. The part of the story I really marveled over, though, was that Christine told it nine months after the fact. Such a small act. Kindness left a sweet impression long after the immediate need had passed.

Let me offer sweet words of encouragement to someone today.
Amen

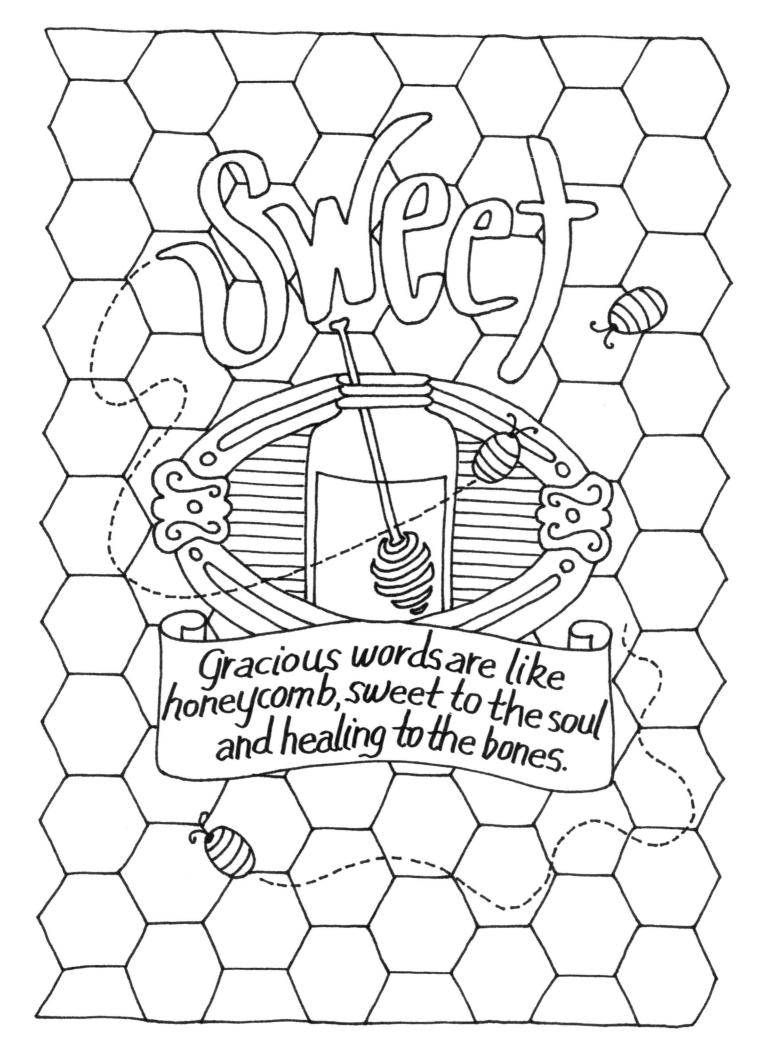

Sweet

Gracious words are like honeycomb, sweet to the soul and healing to the bones.

Laugh-Out-Loud Funny!

*It is cheerful to God when you rejoice or
laugh from the bottom of your heart.*
Dr. Martin Luther King Jr.

D r. Martin Luther King Jr. with the giggles? Is that an image you can even put in your head? I'm not sure
I can. But the man who had a dream, who helped lead the civil rights movement in the 60s, had laughter in his heart. For all the serious business of race relations, of marching, of toiling for justice, here is a
comment about mirth.

This is a reminder, from a man with a heavy responsibility, that a little thing like laughter makes God
smile. And I suspect God likes it even more when we share those moments of joy and laughter. Negative
people are no fun to be around. Changing the mood with a few giggles may seem frivolous but what an uplift
of love. It's fun to be happy! And others want to be around positive people.

I can tell you from experience, smiles and laughter are healing. When I was 15, my dad was dying of a
brain tumor. Through the summer dad was in a hospital bed in our dining room. Yes it was sad to watch my
dad wasting away, but my family said some of the funniest (darkest, most inappropriate) things that summer.
Even when my dad could no longer speak we had him smiling at our crazy way of handling the situation. We
laughed at death, not every day and certainly not at the final hour, but laughter had its place that summer. It
helped us cope. God used laughter. In our family, He brought the giggles when we really didn't think there
was anything to laugh about.

And that is why I love this quote: God wants us to find joy in our lives. There will be struggle and plenty
of it but we can't take ourselves so seriously there isn't room for the laughter of rejoicing.

*Whatever today brings, I want to find a giggle somewhere . . .
and if it can be a side-splitting belly laugh so much the better!
Amen*

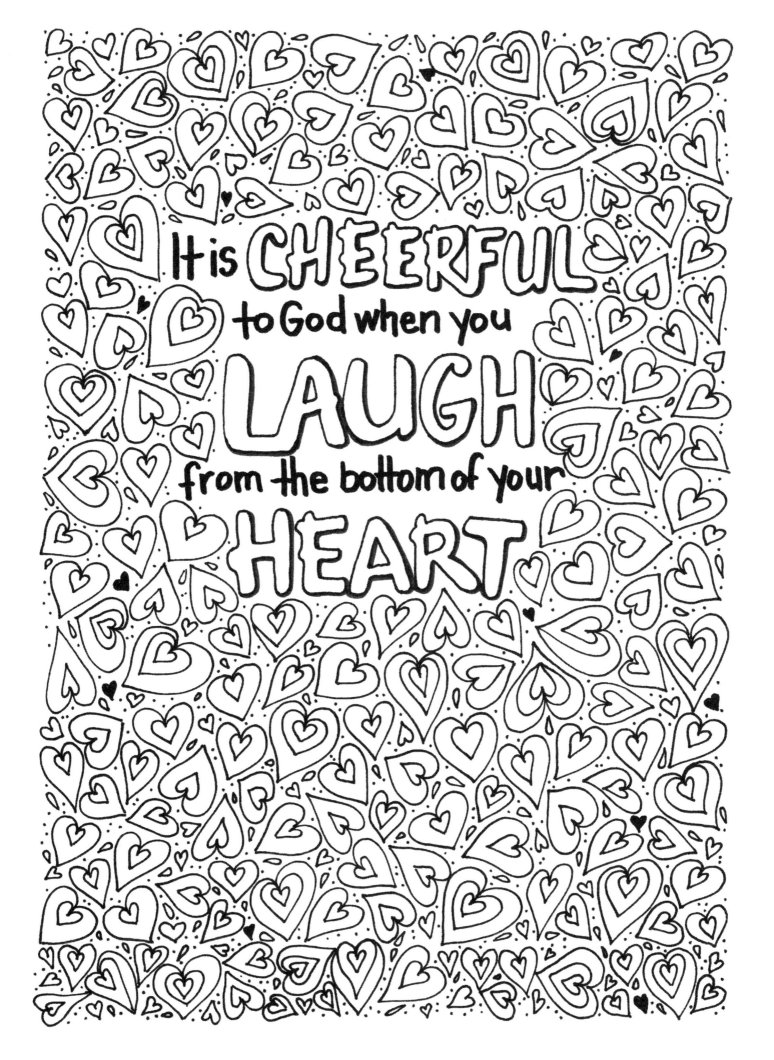

Little Gift, Big Deal

Here's a word of hope in dark times. God meets us where we are even if we aren't looking in His direction; He is always looking in ours.

Liz Curtis Higgs

Most creative people go through dark times of doubt. We wonder if we are making the most of the creativity we feel we've been given as a gift. I wondered if I have anything worthwhile to write? Is this my work or just a successful hobby? I worried.

I annually attend the Mount Hermon Christian Writers Conference in California. It's a great place to learn the writing craft and connect with those in the publishing industry. (And I've been going so long it's also a week I get to see my writer buddies.) Each year I come away with some nugget that motivates me to continue on my creative path. But one year I didn't even want to attend. I felt dry creatively. No lesson could fix that. I didn't want anyone to discover my emptiness.

Each year I take a different course of instruction: non-fiction writing, article writing, marketing. So that year I signed up for something different, public speaking.

Glenna Salsbury taught our class. She's in the speaker hall of fame. She made it look so easy. But she also made those speaking skills accessible. Glenna gently encouraged each student in just the right way. She did not intimidate or badger; she showed each of us how to improve from where we started.

For one exercise, early in the week, she asked each of us to stand up and state our core message. "What is the one thing you want your readers to get from your writing?" As my turn approached, I got more and more anxious. I listened as my classmates presented big ideas with passion. One student wanted to bring vision care to third-world countries. Another talked about the need to stop human trafficking. Still another wanted to address teen pregnancy. I felt very small.

"What is your core message, Lisa?" I hesitated and then practically whispered, "Be kind and smile more?" Glenna smiled. "That's a great message. Don't we all need the reminder to take joy in our lives and share that with others." I straightened up a little. We do all need that reminder. It's no small thing to be kind and keep a positive outlook. Especially in the face of such big issues everyone else is trying to tackle.

The rest of the week I learned more about sticking to my core message. I discovered I could give the world my small idea for the very reason that it was my big passion. God met me in my despair over my writing gifts and helped me move forward. I embraced my message. What once seemed like an insignificant thought has become what I most want to share. Years later it is still the thing I return to when I get lost in my writing (and life).

Hard times come in all shapes and sizes. There are any number of ways we get lost and turn our focus from a God-centered life. But there is hope, the hope of knowing God will seek us out and find us wherever we are looking.

You may not be looking His way, but God has His eye on you today.

Amen

God

meets us where we are.

Even if we aren't looking in His direction,

Hope

He is always looking in ours.

Think On This

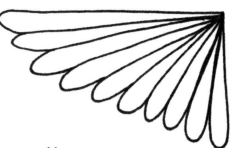

Finally, brothers and sisters, whatever is true, whatever is noble,
whatever is right, whatever is pure, whatever is lovely,
whatever is admirable—if anything is excellent or praiseworthy—think about such things.

Philippians 4:8

I've watched a lot of television in my life. I grew up with *I Love Lucy, The Andy Griffith Show, The Dick Van Dyke Show, The Brady Bunch, The Partridge Family,* and many more. As a teen I watched *M*A*S*H, All in the Family,* and *Love American Style.*

Today I still watch television. Fall is one of my favorite seasons, and not just because it's finally sweater weather again. It's time to cozy up for an evening of new entertainment. September used to be the time of year when all the news shows came out. I would finally know what the characters had been doing all summer or some cliffhanger would at last be resolved. But nowadays you can binge watch your favorites on all kinds of platforms. All the episodes are out at once—no waiting.

Several years ago, leading up to the new season of *The Sopranos,* the network ran the whole first season in a week. Every night there were back-to-back-to-back episodes. I started watching to catch up and get ready to join all the fans eager to see what would occur next. I watched two nights. But something strange happened. The next day I heard all that foul language in my head. I don't curse like they did on the show, but I could hear it in my ear. I just knew at the wrong moment one of those expletives would cross my lips. I was hearing the recording in my head, and it was hard to drown out. Those ugly sounds are not who I am.

I had filled my head with all the wrong stuff. I had listened to too much harsh content. So I gave up the Sopranos. In fact I gave up television for a while. If something as benign as a television show could get in my head and make me feel that uncomfortable, I knew I had to cut it out. The things I listen to or read or ponder have an impact on me.

It is true then what Paul writes in this verse to the Philippians: *Think on whatever is right and noble and lovely and pure.* Then those things will infuse your life. They will be the things that leak out of you. If we think on rotten things then trash is what we will get out of our thinking. I want to treasure the lovely not wallow in the muck. Today I am a little more careful when I select my TV viewing. What we fill our minds with really does matter.

Remind me to fill my thoughts with whatever is true and right and noble
and pure and lovely and admirable so my actions will follow.
Amen

Noticing the Details

This is my Father's world . . .
In the rustling grass I hear Him pass;
He speaks to me everywhere.

Maltbie Davenport Babcock

"This Is My Father's World" is my mom's favorite hymn, and so it is one of my favorites too. She smiles every time it is a selection on Sunday morning, and she hums it often. I am a hummer, too, and so the rhymes reverberate in my head: "All nature sings and round me rings the music of the spheres."

And my favorite line: "In the rustling grass I hear Him pass." God is as close as a breath of wind, touching my cheek and walking beside me. That is the very kind of refreshment I seek when I go out for a walk. Think of that kind of intimacy. How amazing! And yet even with this lyrical reminder I sometimes rush off for a walk. I am getting some exercise. I walk to check off another box on my to-do list. And then there is my competitive reason: to accumulate steps on my Fitbit! Sigh.

Yes, keeping my body healthy is a good thing. However keeping my spirit healthy is a better thing. Going for a walk used to be my quiet time. I used to notice all kinds of details and marvel over the gifts God showers on this world. But when I speed walk, I never quiet my mind long enough to see the details.

So I am slowing down. I am going out for a quiet walk. I am going to look at the fall colors or notice the spring buds. I am going to take a different path so I can see the world anew. I am going to actually stop and smell the roses. For when my spirit is quiet, I can be refreshed. Then is the time God can whisper insights and point out the stuff of life that really matters. The thing that really matters, by the way, is time with God.

Let me find a patch of green today.
Slow me down long enough to sink into Your natural world, Father.
It's amazing!
Amen

Stand Up

Life is like a ten-speed bicycle. Most of us have gears we never use.
Charles M. Schultz

Charles Schultz, the creator of the *Peanuts* cartoon strip, was a quiet man from Minnesota. In 1963, with *Peanuts* in umpteen daily newspapers, CBS and Coca-Cola asked Schultz to create a television Christmas special. What they didn't realize was they'd hired a man who would stick to his creative ideas and to his Christian faith.

Schultz's friend, Lee Mendelson, was the producer of the project. He suggested they use the music of the Vince Guaraldi jazz trio. Schultz loved this idea. (It's hard to imagine *Peanuts* without hearing the Linus and Lucy theme song in your head.) The special ended up having traditional Christmas hymns as well as Beethoven and jazz, which was an unusual mix for a children's cartoon. But then this was never going to be just a kids' show.

Music was not the only way the project was different from others at the time. Schultz wanted children as the characters' voiceovers rather than actors pretending to be children. And the animation had to be right as well. Bill Melendez was hired after he auditioned some drawings. Schultz wanted to be sure his characters still looked right, not some 3-D version far removed from his own print work.

But the biggest way Schultz stuck to his vision was when he put a long Bible passage in the middle of the show. The whole message of the production focused on the true meaning of Christmas. And what better place to find an accurate account of the birth of Christ than the Gospel of Luke? Linus has the now famous scene of taking center stage and explaining the meaning of Christmas to Charlie Brown. This had never been done before on television.

At an initial screening, CBS and Coca-Cola were not pleased with the show. Because it was scheduled to air in a week, they had to show it but didn't order any more work. The rest is history, of course. *The Charlie Brown Christmas Special* has been a part of the holidays for decades, broadcast each year. And the creative team of Schultz, Mendelson, and Melendez went on to produce more than forty-five *Peanuts* specials.

Charles Schultz stuck to his faith and creative convictions with that first show. He didn't change his message for CBS or Coke or anyone when they thought the show was flat and not going to receive high ratings.

I have never been asked to share my faith with millions. But I am asked to share my faith in smaller ways, and I still back down sometimes. I feel the social pressure not to rock the boat or to stay politically correct, or not to push my convictions on others. I don't want to look uncool. When, in fact, I think Jesus is the coolest. He's saved me. Yet I don't always stand up to be counted.

I confess it gets easier to claim Christ the older I get. I suspect it's the wisdom of age. I don't care as much what others think of me. I care what I can do for Christ, how I can stand with Him rather than sit silently. Like Charles Schultz, I want to be able to say that I used all the gears God gave me.

Give me a chance to share my faith today. And give me a brave heart
to answer that call in a way that makes you smile.
Amen

Passion

She [gathers] wool and flax and works with eager hands.

Proverbs 31:13

This is my verse. I was tickled when I found a knitting verse in the bible. Well, you can stretch this verse to mean knitting, and I do. I love to knit! It is my daily habit. I love the feel of fiber on my fingers. Knitting gives me such peace to sit, relax, and create. The benefits seems limitless to me. I make gifts for others and garments for my own wardrobe. I play with my friends at knit night. I use my creative juices to put color and pattern together. I pursue this pastime with enthusiasm.

Knitting is my gift. It comes from God. I think He placed this passion in my heart. I have eager hands because He put a happy habit in my life. You may not be a knitter, but there is probably something in your life that you too pursue with eager hands. Some hobby you love, charity you work for, cause you care about or pastime you enjoy.

These things are gifts from God. He puts desires in our hearts. I think those desires are there for us to find fulfilling work and outlets for our creativity. A well-balanced spreadsheet, a lovingly prepared meal, a perfect golf swing, a smooth-running car engine—all these and many more are passions put in the heart. Ways to find creative outlets. God knows we need fulfilling ways to fill our time. Just getting by is not a joyful way to live. And this is just for the joy of the activity. Hiking for fun is a fine thing to do. Reading new books is an end unto itself. You have been given passions. Go after them! Gather your materials whatever they may be and set to work with joy and eagerness. It will fill your time. It will also fill your heart.

Thank You for the joy of doing,
the fulfillment of creating, and the love of life.
Amen

She gathers wool and flax and works with eager hands

People Watching

Love isn't a state of perfect caring. It is an active noun like struggle.
To love someone is to strive to accept that person exactly the way he or she is right here and now.
Mr. Rogers

I like to people watch. It's amusing and surprising. I work part time in a little knit shop. While sitting at the counter in the shop, I can look out the window and watch the world go by. The shop is at a busy intersection so there is a lot to watch—mom's pushing strollers, business men in pairs walking to lunch, tourists peeking in windows. I sometimes make up stories about the people I see. Of course I'd rather wait on customers in the shop. But on slow days I sit and knit, and I watch the crosswalk right outside the door. I try to guess who might stop in the shop.

The other week a very tall bald man in full motorcycle leathers was waiting to cross the street. He carried a huge helmet under his arm. *Well, he's not stopping in the shop.* The light changed. He crossed the street, opened the shop door, walked right up to the counter, and said "I lost my crochet hook. I need another H hook to finish the project I've started." I'm glad I was sitting down! I did not expect that statement to come out of his mouth.

Appearances can be so deceiving. Who knew a big tattooed biker practiced the gentle art of crochet? I later found this verse that captures the essence of how we should deal with our assumptions about appearance: *But the LORD said to Samuel, "Do not consider his appearance or his height, for I have ejected him. The LORD does not look at the things people look at. People look at the outward appearance, but the LORD looks at the heart (1 Samuel 16:7).* Your heart. God sees into the core of who we are. He sees from the perfect perspective and loves us, faults and all. We are called to try and do the same for each other.

How can you tell just by looking at someone who is surviving a bad day and who is celebrating good news? Should I pick and choose who I am going to be kind to based on appearance alone? If I am only kind to those who "look" like they need it, I am missing opportunities to care for others. Everyone needs a little love. Everyone deserves my acceptance. This is the struggle I attempt by following God's example. And I can only master it by asking for God's help.

Today let me see others as You see them,
with the eyes of love.
Amen

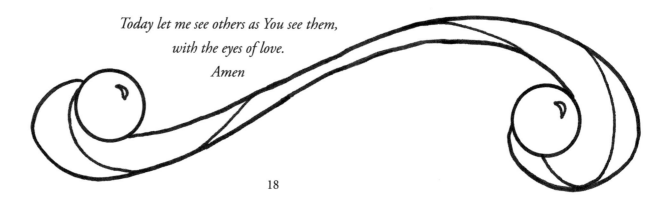

Love isn't a state of perfect caring. It is an active noun like struggle. To love someone is to strive to accept that person exactly the way she is right here and now.

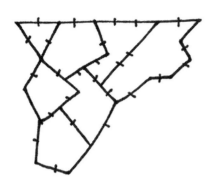

Hundreds,
Thousands,
Millions

The Lord said, "You are precious and honored in my sight, and . . . I love you."

Isaiah 43:4

Walking down Fifth Avenue in Manhattan, I looked around and realized: God knows each one of these people intimately. He loves each one individually. He created every single one of us! God Himself is made of love. I had forgotten these facts as I rushed about my daily business.

When I moved to New York City, the vast numbers of people I saw every day made me realize I had no idea how God can do it. How can He love all these people? There are so many. According to the 2013 U.S. Census, the population of New York City is 8,405,837! Even while walking the busy streets of the city, I can't imagine that number. Nothing puts it in perspective.

To be in the city and walk the avenues is to be reminded of how small I am and how important it is to be kind. With so many people packed in a tight place, a little kindness helps keep the peace. Sure, New Yorkers have a reputation for being rough and fast paced. But, living in the city, I found small courtesies all the time. Someone holds a door. Someone offers directions to the lost. Someone offers to carry a heavy bag up from the train platform. Someone picks up a dropped item and returns it. Someone even pointed out to me when my backpack was hanging open on the subway. Niceties that remind me I am cared for even in a big city.

God loves each person in this city, and the next county and the state beyond that and the country after that and on around the world. I am not the first to notice the enormity of God, but watching the flow of people walk on Fifth Avenue does begin to put into perspective just how many, many, many people God loves. And He shines care on each one of them, including me.

I have a fraction of God's love to offer, and I can still be stingy with it. Living in Manhattan I am trying to give loving-kindness instead of marching through the streets with a frown on my face. It does feel better to smile now and then and offer a helping hand. And with eight million neighbors I have lots of opportunities.

God, You know me by name and care for me personally. The stranger next to me is equally important.
Remind me You care for every person I meet today.
Amen

Sharing the Harvest

But the fruit of the Spirit is love, joy, peace, forbearance, kindness,
goodness, faithfulness, gentleness and self-control.
Against such things there is no law.
Galatians 5:22–23

Like Paul, I am a letter writer. I love the old-fashioned snail mail system. Don't get me wrong; I am techno savvy and can text and email with the best of them. But when I really want to pour out my heart on the page or offer lasting encouragement, I sit down and write a letter or send a card.

My love affair with friendly mail started one Lenten season when, rather than give up something, I decided to add a discipline. I wrote a letter a day. The habit stuck, and that year I sent out more than 500 letters. I have slacked off since then. But I love to encourage my friends through the postal system. Whenever someone in my life is going through a tough time, I send cards and letters. I keep sending them for months at a time. Yes, even in this age of instant communication.

Paul was the same way, sending letters of encouragement and instruction. He wrote to all the churches he loved. He corresponded with the Romans, Corinthians, Galatians, Ephesians, Colossians, Thessalonians, and with Timothy and Titus. Just getting a letter from one place to another in the ancient world was no small task. With no postal service, Paul had to pay couriers or have followers hand deliver his letters over long distances. It took a lot of effort for him to stay connected to all those early churches.

Christianity in its infancy needed shepherding, and Paul was one of the men passionately expending his life to deliver the Good News. Spreading the gospel is a life work, not a campaign that ends at the conclusion of a season or a year. Paul's letter writing left a legacy we still read and use today for instruction and encouragement. His description of the fruit we bear when we are in communion with the Spirit is one example that guides each of us in how to live.

My card writing will not become a collection read by millions of people years from now. My letter writing is meant for the heart of a few. Sharing my faith and love in a letter is an easy way to offer encouragement to those I care about. It's tangible comfort in times of need. It's a card to celebrate times of joy or sorrow. It's sharing life with those far away.

And time is all it takes. Time to stop and think of others. Time to buy a card. Time to search for the mailing address, hunt for a stamp, and drop the letter in the mail. All that is time well spent when the thoughts of encouragement arrive. Paul knew he was spending his time wisely by encouraging young churches. I know I can spare some time to write to loved ones. Are there some small ways you can spend your time today in the service of others as you bear the fruit of the Spirit?

The Spirit has blessed me with so many fruits. Let me share the harvest today.
Amen

The Fruit of the Spirit is Love Joy Peace Patience Kindness Goodness

Look at It This Way . . .

Be Thou my vision, O Lord of my heart
Waking or sleeping, Thy presence my light.
Dallan Forgaill

Be thou my vision. Let me look at the world the way You do, Lord. Let me seek the good instead of the ugly. *Be my best thought both day and night.* Let me concentrate on whatever is positive rather than what is negative. This Irish folk tune turned hymn is a powerful reminder to look at the world the way God does. And it's a tune that gets stuck in my head often. It is a fine "problem" to have as it becomes a reminder to see life from God's perspective.

I am a glass-half-full kind of gal, looking on the bright side of life. I try to see the happy not the crummy. I've been accused of wearing rose-colored glasses. Oh I see the ugly, but I try to look beyond it to the good side.

One thing I find myself doing a lot these days is praying for people in line. I live near New York City, and there are lines everywhere for all kinds of things: getting on the subway, crossing the street, finding a parking place, shopping in stores, waiting in museums, buying groceries. And there is always someone who is pretty cranky about being stuck waiting.

I get annoyed with the wait too. I am tempted to take out my phone so I can play games or check my email, anything to distract myself from the situation. I want to block out everyone around me. However lately while standing in line, I pray for those around me. I seek out whoever is grumpiest, complaining the loudest, or just looks the most defeated.

My prayer does not immediately bring calm to my surroundings, but it brings calm to me. It helps me have compassion for those nearby. I am no longer disconnected; I am engaged, taking an active part in making the situation better just by holding people up in prayer. Prayer is my secret weapon at those times. It's a good practice. And just when I am the one about to get grumpy, that little Irish tune will pop in my head.

Be my vision, Father. Let me see with my heart.
Amen

Yours the Glory

I confess I belittle God. I make Him small. I humanize Him to the point where sometimes He's my best friend not my King. He created the universe, and it's amazing that He knows my name. In my humanness I can't comprehend Him fully so I do what humans do; I try to make Him understandable. And I fail. I get comfortable with His small size in my life. He is big, more powerful than I can fathom. It's kind of scary actually, and that's my excuse for making Him my size. But I lose. I lose the awe and the greatness that makes Him King.

In an effort to understand God's grandeur, I looked closer at the words in the verse from First Chronicles: glory, majesty, splendor. I found a wide range of synonyms. They helped me better see how spectacular God was being described. When I looked up "exalted," these words came up: exaggerated, inflated, pretentious. When I searched "glory," I found celebrity. And when I searched "majesty," I got words like "severity" and "polish."

I began to see that for each word I read in the verse, the descriptions of God used only the positive definitions. There was not a negative in the bunch. God's glory is not from celebrity but from power. His exaltation is not pretentious; it is very real. God is larger than life. Synonyms are the best we have to try and describe the unknowable. God is great but loves the little. He is power but wields it with wisdom. He gets the glory because only He is worthy.

All our positive adjectives fall short. Majesty, splendor, exalted. Those are words you reserve only for a King. Our King. The King. I may not be able to comprehend the awe of my King, but that is the very reason to try. God is owed my reverence.

You are exalted head over all, God.
Let me sit quietly with this thought and rejoice.
Amen

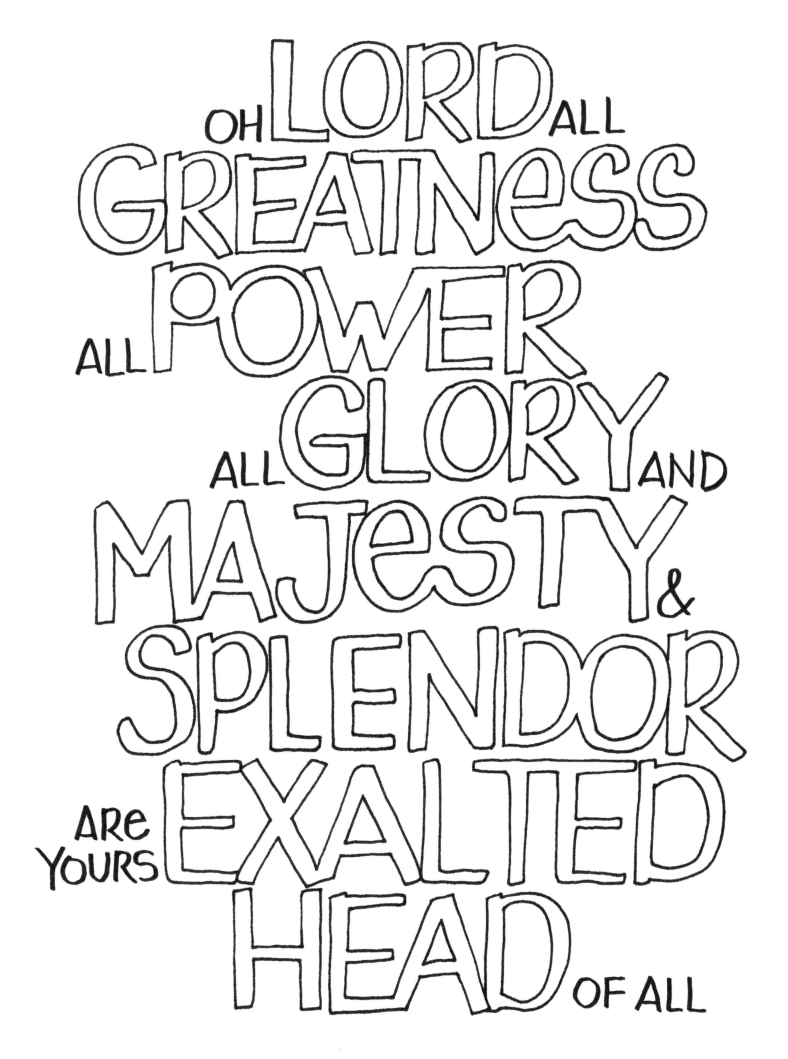

Surprised by Sparkles

What people call serendipity sometimes is just having your eyes open.

Jose Manual Barroso

We arrived at the Denver rail station early in the morning, ready to climb aboard our train headed up into the Rocky Mountains. My in-laws, husband, son, and I were having a little winter get-away. This would be a fun trip through snow-covered vistas on our way up to Glenwood Springs. But our train had been delayed leaving Chicago the day before. The California Zephyr would not pull in until early afternoon. All five of us slumped next to our luggage. Now what?

We stashed our luggage at the station and took off to explore downtown Denver. We ended up at the Tattered Cover Bookstore. The store is nearly a city block full of books. That kept us busy all morning. We checked in at the station. New arrival estimate: 5 p.m. *Bummer.* We headed back downtown for a leisurely lunch; we had the time! We passed away the afternoon browsing around the little shops downtown.

Finally at four o'clock we headed back to the station. The new arrival estimate: 8 p.m. *What!* We had exhausted our shopping and dining in Denver. We each pulled out a book from our early morning shopping spree and settled in to wait some more.

This was not turning out to be the beautiful, snow-covered train ride through the Rocky Mountain scenery that I'd envisioned when I booked the trip. It was all ruined. I was so disappointed. I read my book to take my mind off things.

Finally at 8:05 p.m., a full 13 hours late, the California Zephyr pulled into the station. We boarded and found our coach seats. The lights in the car were on as we settled into our seats. But as the train pulled out of the station, the car went dark except for a few safety lights. *Perfect. Now we can't even read our books.* I stared out the window into the black night. The train started climbing into the foothills. *We are missing all the dramatic views.* I pouted.

Look at that! My mother-in-law pointed out the window. There was a house all lit up with Christmas lights. A house so far up in the foothills you could only see this display of lights from the train. It made me smile as we chugged by. Up ahead there was another farmhouse all lit up. Ten minutes later we passed another. And so it went. The three-hour trip up to Glenwood Springs was dotted with ranch after farmhouse after cabin all decked out in holiday sparkles. We never would have seen any of it if we came up in the daylight.

My grumbling about a ruined trip finally reversed when I opened my eyes to the sparkle of some Christmas lights. I laughed at myself. I looked back on a day filled with delights: unexpected food and fun. Rather than be cranky I finally saw the joy not the hassle. It took all day for me to really see it, but there was fun. I wonder, what else do I miss when I grouse rather than make the best of things? There might be some sparkles I overlook.

May I embrace the unexpected today with a sense of joy and adventure
rather than annoyance and frustration.

Amen

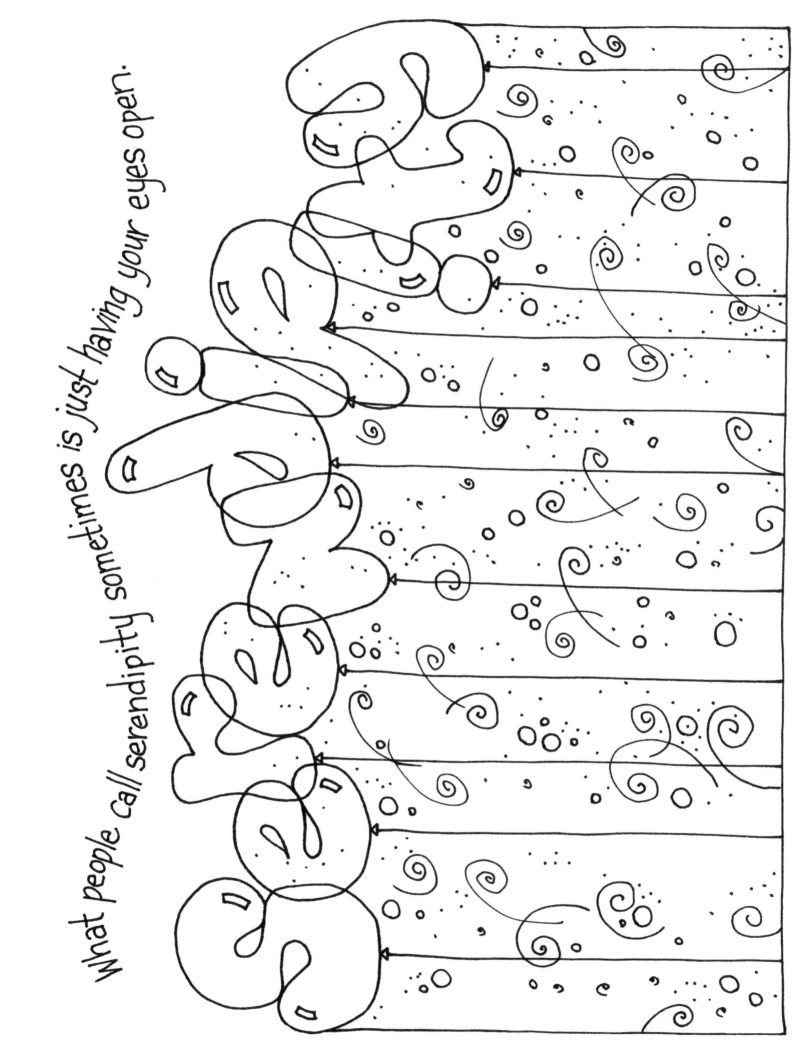

What people call serendipity sometimes is just having your eyes open.

I Got This

It was my son's babysitter Lydia who shared this verse with me years ago. As a teen Lydia took comfort in these words. Finding your way in the world is tough at any age. But knowing God has your back brings some peace. It is sometimes only in hindsight that we see the plan as God knew it from the beginning.

I know Lydia had big plans for her life. She studied dance from the age of six. Her focus was to perform on stage, the most creative form of artistic expression she could imagine. I got in touch with her recently to see how her plans unfolded.

After graduation Lydia danced professionally with several companies in Houston, Texas, and she married her college sweetheart. Then Lydia's husband got a career opportunity in Virginia. The couple decided to relocate; this was a big position for Jonathon. Lydia went, but her dance career had been on the verge of blossoming and now she felt banished to a place with little opportunity. "I thought it was the death of my career." But as you guessed, God had other plans for her.

While dancing in Houston, Lydia discovered she was the dancer in the troupe with ideas to share with the choreographers and artistic directors. But they saw her as an instrument, a piece to be moved gracefully in their creation, not a collaborator. It was hard for her to keep quiet. Now that she was in a new location, maybe there were new ways to express her creativity.

In Virginia, Lydia did what any young person does in a new town; she googled opportunities to see what was going on. She typed in dance, and she found Halestone's Community Dance Connection Theater. She became a Visiting Artist at the theater. She also found a mentor/collaborator. For two years Lydia watched the head of the company lead in ways that included the community and shared dance with all ages and skill levels. She got to dance, but she also got to create and teach. "I was surprised to find such creative expression off stage. I had always assumed my life as a dancer would be performing."

The move to Virginia turned out not to be permanent. Jonathon was offered an opportunity to return to Houston. This time Lydia did not seek a company to join. She had a new dream, to continue the work she discovered in Virginia. She started her own dance company, Frame.

It took time and climbing the learning curve, but now Lydia runs a non-profit business. She is not dancing on stage full time, but she is doing much, much more. Her creativity has blossomed in a way she never imagined. She writes grants, teaches, choreographs, and brings dance to her community in creative ways that fill her heart and the hearts of those whose lives she now blesses. Yes, Lydia still steps on stage with the joy of movement she felt as a little girl, but now she is living the bigger dream God has planned for her.

I'm holding onto Your promise of a plan for my future.
Thank You for caring for me so deeply.

Amen

Sunny Mail

Try to be a rainbow in someone's cloud.

Maya Angelou

In 2004 our whole extended family gathered in Hudson, Wisconsin, to celebrate my Grammy Mabel's 100th birthday. It was a grand weekend. A reporter from the *Hudson Star Observer* covered the event. This was big news in a town of 6,000 people. He asked Mabel how she'd managed to live to be 100. She said it was because she was stubborn. We all laughed but it was true; Mabel came from strong Norwegian stock.

After the party, as the family was packing up to fly off to different homes, we all commented, "See you next year at the 101st!" Mabel was so vibrant and the center of her day, it was hard to imagine her not making it to her 101st birthday. We all laughed and figured, yes, we'd be back next year.

However, I went home with a heavy heart. The age of 100 is very old after all, triple digits. I might not see Gram again. I lived three times zones and 2,500 miles away. I couldn't exactly stop by for an afternoon cup of tea or a quick hug. But I wanted to keep the joy of her birthday celebration going. Talking on the phone was out; Gram's hearing made that very difficult. And Gram was not a friend of technology, so texting and email were out as well. I decided to send Grammy friendly mail, lots of cards. I planned to write a note every week.

It was actually hard to know what to say. Gram's world was so small. What could I say that would interest her? At first I talked about her party. Then I talked about my son, her great-grandson. Next I wrote memories of visiting her as a kid. Then I wrote about family stories I'd heard of her growing-up years. Eventually I ran out of things to say. But I wanted to keep her mailbox full. I bought more pretty cards and just wrote *I love you* inside.

When Mabel died three months after her 101st birthday, I was given a pile of cards. Grammy had saved her mail, tucked in her comfy chair and stacked on her bedside table. Dozens and dozens of cards—it was a little astonishing to see them all in one pile. I didn't realize how many I'd sent.

I don't think Mabel's days were particularly sad or lonely in her nursing home, but I suspect they might have been a little boring, even if she napped a lot. The cloud at the end of her life was monotony. So it was lovely to see evidence of a little sunshine when I was handed a pile of mail. And it had been so easy for me to do. *I love you, Gram.* Stamp it and drop it in the mail.

Who needs some sunshine today?
Where can I provide some color and happiness?
Amen

Seize the Moment

Seize the moment.
Think of all those women on the Titanic *who waved off the dessert cart.*
Erma Bombeck

Erma Bombeck makes me laugh, the big kind of laughter that makes my sides hurt. She was a humorist who wrote a weekly newspaper column about suburban life from the mid-60s to the late 90s.

When she began writing, the picture of domesticity was sweetness, light, and wearing pearls while vacuuming before making the perfect dinner for four. The reality of course was a little different: "Never have more children than car windows." She was a wise woman. And she also knew: "If you can laugh at it, you can live with it." She let all those gals in the suburbs know they were not alone. Someone else was having just as crazy a day as they were managing the house and kids and food and husband and life! Her take on motherhood and homemaking stands up even today; it's still a crazy pursuit. That's why I love her quote on seizing the moment. She put life in perspective. A little levity points out how important it is to grab onto the important things in life. They are not always going to be here and neither are we.

Erma's readers knew how she had battled and beaten breast cancer with a mastectomy. But she kept secret that she had had polycystic kidney disease from her early twenties and endured daily dialysis for years before her death. Still she seized the moments of her life, appearing on television, writing her daily column, publishing bestsellers, running her home, raising her kids, and making people laugh.

There is another quote of her that captures how she pursued life, "When I stand before God at the end of my life, I would hope that I would not have a single bit of talent left, and could say, 'I used everything you gave me.'" I think Erma Bombeck could say mission accomplished. She lived her life to the full with all the gifts God gave her. I want to follow her example.

Help me seize a moment today and use all my talents.
You have given me the gifts for a full life.
Amen

Rubbing It In

My mother-in-law, Marie, battled cancer at the end of her life. Her kidneys were failing. One of the symptoms was itching. Her whole body itched most of the time. Often she could ignore it with force of will. She did have some medications that helped, but she liked to save those for night, taking them near bedtime so she could sleep. During the day she kept lotion nearby, slathering often to ease the itch.

As her disease progressed, she spent more time in bed. On my last visit to see her, I asked her if I could give her a back rub. "I'll rub some lotion where you can't reach." She smiled. "Sure." It helped us both. I knew I was saying good-bye. "How bout a foot rub too?" "That would be nice." I lotioned her toes and rubbed till she fell asleep. I happily gave her a foot rub every day of my visit. It was a comfort to both of us.

I knew when I left it was my last visit. I could just feel it. I still kept in touch of course. And when Marie got too weak to talk on the phone, I would text her best friend Jonna to get an update. I felt helpless being so far away even though I knew Marie was well cared for. I just wanted to rub her feet one more time. So one day I did.

In my mind's eye I took the time to rub her feet. I caressed each toe. I smoothed over both heels. I pressed my thumb into the arch of her foot. It took me half an hour to imagine the whole massage.

The next day I got a phone call from Jonna. She was so happy to report that Marie had had a really good day yesterday. I was happy to hear it, but sad I hadn't been there to share it with her. I teared up and wished I could see her one more time. I told Jonna about my mental foot rub.

She said the kindest thing to me, "I know that helped. I know that God used that gift of love as a prayer to help Marie have a good day. God can bend time and space to His whim." I want to believe that Jonna is right. God has ways of moving in this world we can't even imagine. He uses all the prayers of our hearts even when it's a long-distance foot massage.

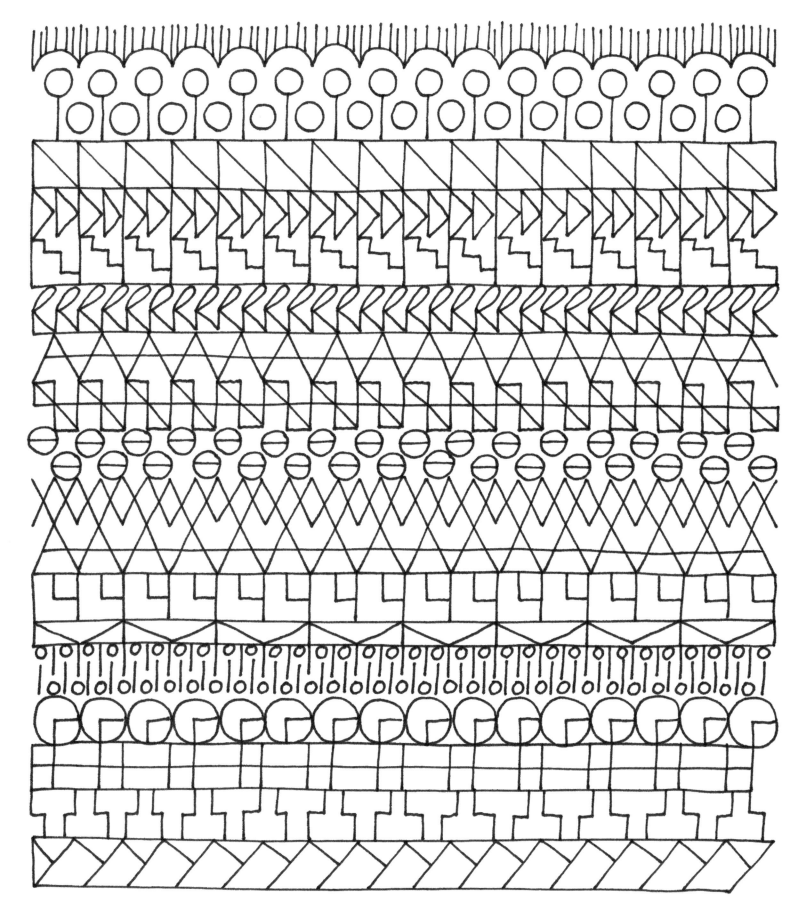

PONDER ANEW
WHAT THE ALMIGHTY CAN DO

Surrounded

Christ beside me, Christ before me,
Christ behind me, Christ within me,
Christ beneath me, Christ above me.
Saint Patrick

Saint Patrick's words sink deeply into my soul. I need the reminder of his words: Christ surrounding me so effectively I can't move without Him. Because, if I'm honest, I move without Christ all too often. I slip by. I take a shortcut. I forget to stay Christ-centered.

Saint Patrick wanted to keep Christ at the core of his being. I want that too. Saint Patrick had to work at it just like I do.

Patrick may be the patron saint of Ireland, but he was born in England in AD 387, a time of wars and kingdom fighting. He was captured by the Irish and forced into a life of servitude when he was just 16 years old. He came from a deeply religious family, and I suspect this served him well while he was indentured. Eventually he escaped and returned home. But something drew him back to Ireland as a missionary.

What could make a man return to a land where he'd been humiliated and forced into servitude? The only answer I see is Christ. God asked Patrick to return, and he answered the call. He went back to the people who had treated him poorly, but he did not return alone. Patrick returned with Christ before him, paving the way. Christ beside him, traveling the road. And Christ within him, keeping him centered on the heavenly task. His job was no less than to bring the gospel to Ireland.

I used to think of Saint Patrick as the reason we had to wear green every March 17th to avoid getting pinched. However, looking further into his life, I found a man who went where Christ would have him go. And he went with the assurance that he would not be alone. Patrick was protected on all sides by Christ. And so are we.

I don't want to do anything that is apart from Your will.
Grant me the grace to follow You closely today.
Amen

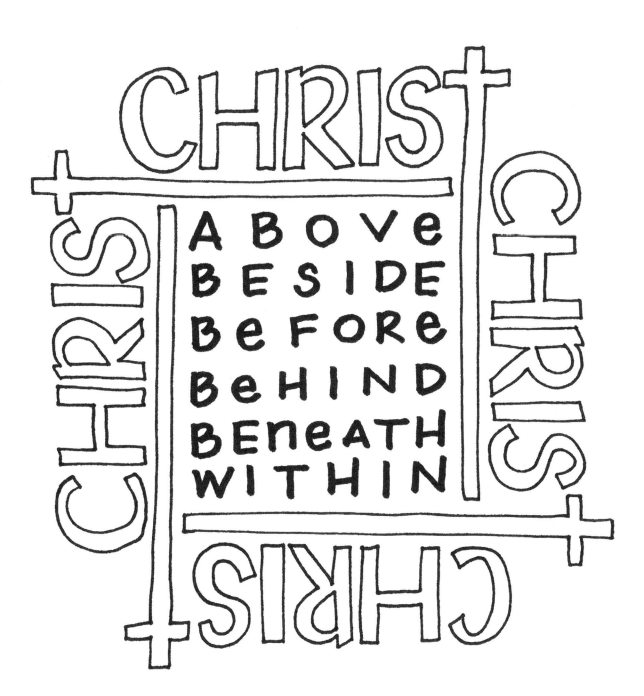

CHRIST
CHRIST
CHRIST
CHRIST

ABOVE
BESIDE
BEFORE
BEHIND
BENEATH
WITHIN

Little Influence

Joy is the net of love by which we can catch souls.
Mother Teresa

Tiny beginnings. Sometimes I bemoan the small impact I seem to be making on the world. I want to do good work and help the world be a better place. But my sphere of influence is narrow. What difference can I possibly make? Why would God even want to use me? Do you ever feel this way? Small. Then I think of insignificant beginnings and small efforts given in love. They make all the difference in my perspective.

Mother Teresa was born in Macedonia, a small country on the world stage. She was a little woman, physically only 4 feet 11 inches. She started the Missionaries of Charity with just 13 women. Tiny. From these meager beginnings Mother Teresa's work and influence grew. Her message was to love the unlovable. To show those who had been cast aside, literally, they are loved by God. Sometimes this was by helping them die with dignity in a clean place. Not exactly the way to gather a huge following.

Yet by the time of Mother Teresa's death in 1997, after 70 years of ministry, there were 4,000 sisters and 300 brothers operating in 610 missions in 123 countries. There was nothing small about the growth of love coming from the Missionaries of Charity.

Even as I recount these numbers I suspect you are still feeling inadequate. And it's true they are daunting numbers; thousands and thousands of people have been and still are influenced by Mother Teresa. What chance have you and I to make such an impact? Think of this though: Of all the people she helped, not all of them knew she was famous in the world of ministry. All that one person knew was the love of someone caring for them at their bedside. That matters and had a huge impact to them.

It is hard to love someone we hardly know, but this is something we can do. We can begin in our own neighborhoods, loving and caring about the people next door. Sometimes we don't even know the names of those around us. So the perfect place to start is an introduction. It may never lead to world recognition, but it will lead to that one person knowing they are loved and seen by God.

Mother Teresa didn't set out to conquer the world. She only meant to ease the suffering of those around her. She wanted to make sure those she could see knew they were loved. A simple beginning of small tasks worked over a lifetime. And that's the key: work over a lifetime. Mother Teresa didn't stop. She kept going day after day after day. The only way to do that is to call on God for help. This is a model I can follow, calling on God daily. He will set out the small task I can accomplish, and it will have all the influence He needs in the world.

There are no small tasks in the world.
Show me the little ways I can make a big difference in someone's life today.
Amen

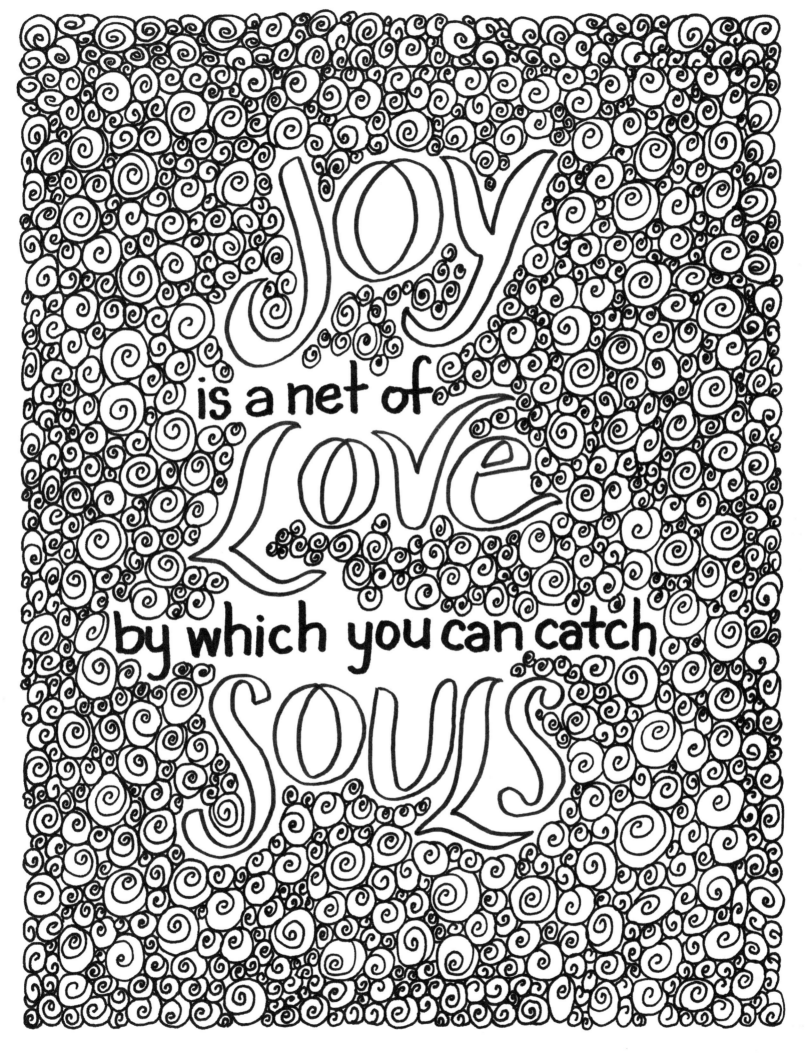

Counting My Blessings

Thou shalt rejoice in every good thing
which the LORD thy God has given unto thee.
Deuteronomy 26:11 KJV

When life is treating you rough, it's always a good idea to count your blessings. But in that moment it can be hard. If you are like me, you start off with the easy stuff. These are the things you know you should be thankful for and may have forgotten are gifts from God: health, home, enough to eat, and clothes to wear. The basics. Then I try to expand my thankfulness.

I thank God for nature: rainbows, spring rains, mountains majesty, crystal lakes, spectacular fall colors and the list goes on.

I thank God for health: bodies that work, children that grow, elders with wisdom, diseases in remission, medicines to manage pain, and that list goes on.

I thank God for family and friends: relationships that encourage and inspire me, people who love and care for me, friends who make me laugh and giggle, and people given to enrich my life.

I thank God for work to do: purposes to pursue, jobs to fulfill, harvests to reap, causes to champion, and an unending array of challenges.

All these sound so grand and wonderful, and they are! But I got to thinking there are even more reasons to give thanks. The God of the universe loves me so much He took the time to shower me every day with treasures. I started to compile a list. These are things I probably don't need but make my day so much better. This is the stuff that makes life shine like a new penny (ooo, see, there's another blessing):

Hot chocolate	Jelly beans	Confetti
Snowmen	Whoopie cushions	Helium balloons
Finger puppets	Fireflies	Fireworks
Love songs	Cotton candy	Fall colors
Popcorn	Ladybugs	Toddlers
Flip flops	Cartoons	New yarn
Lattes	Pinkie rings	Naps
Jump ropes	Sand castles	Friendly snail mail

The next time you start to count your blessings, remember to think small. There are tiny bits of goodness sprinkled all over your day. The goodies from God just meant to bring a smile and help you feel as blessed as you are.

Help me think small and see all the tiny ways You love me.

Amen

It Is Well with My Soul

When peace, like a river, attendeth my way,
When sorrows like sea billows roll;
Whatever my lot, Thou hast taught me to say,
It is well, it is well with my soul.

Horatio Spafford

Tragedy piled on Horatio Spafford. First the great Chicago Fire of 1871 consumed much of the city along with many of his real estate holdings and ruined him financially. That same year his four-year-old son died of scarlet fever. Then in 1873 Horatio's wife and four daughters were traveling to Europe by ship when the vessel hit another ship and sank. His wife survived and sent him a now famous telegram, "Saved alone. . . ." Surely all this was more heartache than one man could process or respond to. However Horatio's response is a marvel and thing of beauty. Horatio Spafford penned the words to the great hymn "It is well with my soul."

Knowing the tragic story behind the song makes me tear up nearly every time I sing this hymn. I think one reason I get so emotional about his words is that I admire his response to pain. I do not think I could raise my head to heaven the way he did. Like everyone, I have experienced loss and disappointments in my life, but my first response has not been: *It is well with my soul*. Oh no. I am NOT well. I am angry/sad/confused/hurt/lost. So how could Spafford be well after such tragedies?

The trick is to listen to all his words. In the lyrics he cries out to God for help through his pain. He pleads for peace. He realizes with certainty that God will provide the peace he craves. Why is he certain? He knows because he writes: *Christ hath regarded my helpless estate and hath shed his own blood for my soul.* In his pain Horatio remembered God did not abandon him. God understood the weight of the loss of a child and reminded him that he is saved. Even more, Horatio was able to write the words: *For in death as in life Thou wilt whisper Thy peace to my soul.* This is a man who found comfort even in the midst of terrible loss. Horatio turned toward God rather than away from Him, and it made all the difference.

Every life includes loss. We can cry out to God in each painful situation. Even if our response to tragedy is not acceptance, God is with us. I don't turn my face to God with every disappointment in life and I struggle to find peace. Sometimes the words of a great hymn helps. "It is well" rings with a deep peace only God provides.

Finding my way through life's disappointments is so difficult without You, Father.
Please remind me You are at my side whatever my loss.

Amen

WHEN SORROWS
LIKE SEA BILLOWS ROLL
IT IS WELL WITH
MY SOUL~

Stop.

I sit on my favorite rock, looking over the brook, to take time away from busy-ness, time to be . . .
it's something we all need for our spiritual health, and often we don't take enough of it.

Madeleine L'Engle

You. *You, are going to a silent retreat? Yes, me.* My husband tried hard not to laugh at me. You see I am a bit of a chatterbox. In fact I am not quiet even when I am alone. I hum. I sing. I talk to myself. The thought of being quiet for an entire weekend was a foreign idea to me too. But I didn't want him to know that. I was determined to try.

Life gets overwhelming sometimes, and the thought of being quiet and alone for a whole weekend was enticing. I wanted to recharge. I wanted to reconnect with my spiritual side. Heck, I just wanted to take a nap. But I was nervous. What were the rules going to be?

I should not have worried. The rules, such as they were, were to do my best to connect with God in a new and deeper way. The leaders of the retreat gave us a short guided talk to get us started each morning and afternoon. Basically we had hours and hours of time to just be. It was startling.

It took me an hour to settle into the quiet that first morning. I jumped through so many ideas of how I was supposed to be. I should pray. I should sit quietly. I should meditate. I should read meaningful verses. I laughed: I should get over myself. I think God laughed too. He was just waiting for me to get quiet, really quiet.

In the afternoon I took a long walk and breathed in some clean air. I stopped to sit under a tall redwood. I was finally quiet. I listened. No agenda of prayers, just sitting and thinking the word "God" with a smile on my face. I did not hear God's voice. I did not have a great revelation. What I did eventually feel was a sense of peace and the thought in my head was: *It's okay to stop. It's okay to do nothing but sit in My presence.* Ahhh. What a gift. This is what I came for.

Of course this spiritual check up, or slow down, or whatever you want to call it, did not last. Like any good health practice, I needed to do it periodically to gain the benefits. But having tried silence once, I longed for it again and again. I signed up for the retreat annually. I found being quiet and setting myself apart for a little while really did benefit my spiritual health. I returned to my day-to-day energized and ready for the rush of life, even though I hate the rush. I have more to give those in my world. And I have a little smile on my face, a secret. I know how to get the calm back when life goes nuts again: Quiet. Time away.

Okay fine for her. You are thinking. *But I can't a spend whole weekend in the woods.* Fair enough. But what about an afternoon off? Can you carve out a spot of time to try quiet? A park near your house? A museum with a lovely painting? A closed door to your bedroom? Some place where you can get an hour of time alone. It is an important way to stay healthy. Do not underestimate the value of quiet.

Time away and alone is not a reward; it is a necessity.
I will look for a way to get quiet and recharge with You, dear Father.

Amen

He Is Risen Indeed!

Christ the Lord is risen today,
Alleluia!
Charles Wesley

This is a hymn I have sung every Easter as far back as I can remember. It's a shout to heaven: Hallelujah! Christ is alive! I love this song. It's a celebration of the glory of rescue. Christ has saved us, He bore our burden of sin, and He is risen from the dead. We will get to join Him in glory one day. Wow! That really is cause for singing at the top of your voice. And the words of this hymn fill my soul:

Raise your joys and triumphs high!
Christ hath opened paradise!
Hail the resurrection!

The whole hymn rejoices with exclamation points. But I only ever get to sing it at church once a year. Even Christmas songs get a whole month of airtime. I wish I could be reminded more often of the gift Christ has given me, because I fear complacency.

I can actually forget I am saved. I don't act on all that it means. I am saved means a life infused with Christ. It means a God-centered existence, one filled with seeking His plan for me not insisting on my ideas. Being saved means a life lived with God as my King. I need that reminder more often than I would like to admit.

This hymn carries a message I don't want to hear just once a year. It's a powerful reminder I want to belt out often. It may not be anywhere close to Easter today, but remember: CHRIST THE LORD IS RISEN TODAY!

I will rejoice today in the knowledge that
Christ the Lord is risen! He is risen indeed!
Amen!

CHRIST THE LORD IS RISEN TODAY ALLELUIA

Anchored

When darkness veils His lovely face, I rest in His unchanging grace;
In every high and stormy gale, my anchor holds within the veil.
On Christ the solid rock I stand, all other ground is sinking sand.

Edward Mote

The Solid Rock" is a turbulent hymn. Listen to some of the images presented: *in every high and stormy gale, in the whelming flood, when darkness veils.* It's all pretty grim. And that is just how I feel when I am crashing into deadlines, sinking in to-do lists, and drowning in the everyday stuff that seems to doom me to live a life in panic mode. It doesn't have to be this way. "The Solid Rock" gives us alternatives: *hope built on Jesus, my anchor, on Christ the solid rock I stand.*

Recently I took God up on His promise of grace. I was struggling under a deadline. I needed to finish some writing as well as entertain houseguests for three days. Not a workable combination. To top things off, I was stuck for an idea to finish my work. Help. Somehow in the mist of my worry I decided to take a break, take a breath, and ask for grace. I prayed and reminded myself that nothing—nothing—gets done creatively if I don't have God with me in the process.

I laid it all out for Him. *I have a deadline. I have company coming. I want to play and create with You. Help.* I picked up my colored pencils and doodled. This was nothing related to my writing. I played. And 20 minutes later I felt more calm, and a few ideas came dribbling through. Even better, when I checked my email I found my deadline had been lifted. I had an extra week to complete my work. I let go and rested in God's grace and found calm on the other side.

Sometimes I forget what a solid rock Christ is. Hebrews 13:8 reminds me: *Jesus Christ, the same yesterday, today and forever.* He is solid, unchanging, eternal. I love that about Him, because I'm all over the place. I can trust Him to lift me up and hold me fast in all that I do. So whether struggling with deadlines, worried over finances, or just slogging through the laundry, He is there. He is there when I am admiring the fall colors, delighting in time with my son, or happily sipping a cup of tea. He is always the same. I stand on the solid rock that gives my life a firm foundation, whatever I am doing.

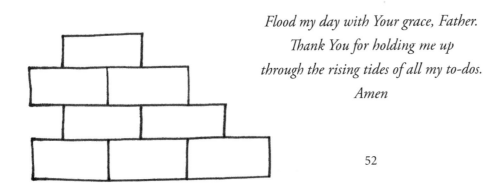

Flood my day with Your grace, Father.
Thank You for holding me up
through the rising tides of all my to-dos.
Amen

I Will Listen

One word or pleasing smile is often enough to raise up a saddened and wounded soul.

Therese of Lisieux

Attending a professional conference can be great fun or feel like one of the most isolating events on your calendar. When you go to one of those gatherings, you have to put on your "game face." You are there to schmooze. Your job is to get information and network. Conferences are high stress, even if you love going and want to be there.

My friend, Harry, told me the story of his recent conference experience.

I go to our industry mid-winter conference every year. I love it. When I was young guy, I couldn't wait to see all my friends. For me it's all about relationship, relationship, relationship. I hated to go to bed, and I couldn't wait to get up. Now I'm old. I can't wait to go to bed, and I hate to get up. But it's still all about relationship for me.

Anyway I'm at the conference, and I run into Josh, a young guy who used to date my daughter. "Hey man! How ya doin?" I asked him. "Not good," he said. "My marriage is in a tough spot and work is bad. Seems my life is coming apart at the seams." My heart went out to the guy. For one thing he was honest enough to tell me how he was really doing. We sat down and talked for a while. I offered him some encouragement. Just letting him talk was enough I think. I was able to pray with him too.

As Josh went off to his next seminar, I ran into Tim, a co-worker from my office. He urged me, "Hey man, come with me to this next seminar. It sounds great." "Nah. I just want to roam the halls." I told Tim what had just happened. "I think there must be other guys here hurting as much as Josh. I want to be open to finding them and see if I could offer a little encouragement." Tim got it and wished me well.

This is a change of heart for me. I had been thinking of this kind of thing for weeks leading up to the conference: the idea of encouragement being key for folks. Putting it into practice with that chance meeting made me want to do more of it. I love to hang out with my buddies at the conference, but I was seeing a new way to build relationship. I wanted to be sure and look for the guys who might need a listening ear or a word of prayer.

I don't remember now if I had anymore significant conversations as I roamed the halls, but I was open and willing to be used. The young guys need us older guys for guidance. So I was willing to forego some of the social schmoozing so I can hang with the guys needing help.

Prick up my ears. Give me an open heart. Let me be the one
willing to listen to someone who needs a little encouragement today.

Amen

By wisdom a house is built and through through knowledge its rooms are filled with

A Tune of Trust

Trust in the LORD with all your heart, and lean not on your own understanding;
in all your ways acknowledge Him, and He shall direct your paths.

Proverbs 3:5–6 NKJV

These words from Proverbs have been set to a lovely piece of music. It's a tune I don't mind getting caught in my head. The comforting words are a helpful reminder to trust. The tune can be sung as a round, where at least three voices sing exactly the same melody, but each voice begins at a different time so the parts coincide in the different voices but nevertheless fit harmoniously together. You know, like "Row, Row, Row Your Boat." I love the challenge of singing rounds, and I love it even more when I get lost in these words and let the music swirl round and fill me. It becomes a prayer.

At choir practice we are good at praying for each other. Part of our rehearsal time is always devoted to prayer requests and then praying aloud for each other. One evening several of us were struggling with tough decisions in our lives. We each asked for discernment, help in figuring our way forward. One of the sopranos suggested we sing these verses from Proverbs as a way to calm our fears and remind us that God is in charge and we can trust Him.

The sopranos and altos started. Then the tenors and basses joined in. The lyrics circled my head, and I took them to heart. I let the music fill me and settle my spirit. *Yes Lord, I will trust You with my life. I don't understand. I can't seem to let go, but I will let You direct my path.* We sang on and on. I saw others in the choir were as moved as I was with this comforting reminder.

Answers didn't come immediately for each of us in choir. There were more prayer evenings at choir rehearsal, but having my friends help me seek understanding through prayer was a huge help as I struggled to give God my whole heart.

Trust is a hard thing to give. We do our best to invite God into our lives. We praise Him for His good care. We acknowledge that He is in control, not us. And we pray for His peace to soften our hearts so we can trust Him all the more.

The melody in my heart wants to trust You.
Help my head to follow this tune as well.
Amen

Tiny Bubbles

Do your little bit of good where you are;
it's those little bits of good put together that overwhelm the world.

Archbishop Desmond Tutu

I switched laundry detergents. With the old brand I put in nearly a third of a cup of liquid. I read the directions on the new brand. I measured a thimble full into the small cap. This could not possibly clean my clothes. I shook my head; this can't be right. But I had switched precisely to be more economical. This jug of detergent was more expensive; however, at this rate it would last so much longer. *But we'll just see if it works.* I set the dials and hit start.

Check it out! I pulled fresh, clean clothes out of the washer and popped them in the dryer. Concentrated power. Amazing. Such a tiny amount of suds made a clean difference. I was reminded of the mustard seed verse. You know the one: *It is like a mustard seed, which is the smallest of all seeds on earth. Yet when planted, it grows and becomes the largest of all garden plants, with such big branches that the birds can perch in its shade* (Mark 4:31). Much comes from tiny beginnings.

Sometimes our efforts to be good, to show the world some kindness, seem pitifully small. What difference does it make to hold open a door or smile at a stranger? How can it possibly matter when we send a card to a friend, take time to call a family member, or make a point of remembering our regular barista's name? But, what if we are the detergent cleaning the world? What if we are the ones who are keeping the chaos at bay? Our small acts of kindness bring a moment of peace and calm to someone's day. Our little bits of good change everything.

Kindness reminds a stranger they are seen. Someone cares for them. Kindness gives you a way to connect the dots with friends and family. Every little act of good will and love share's Christ's love and is a witness of His grace. Today, be the one to add a small measure of good to someone's day. Together we can overwhelm the world.

Let me be the soap that cleans a heart and
brightens the day with an act of loving-kindness.
Amen

82

Do your little bit of good

All those little bits overwhelm the world

Vacation Bible School

Jesus loves me! This I know,
For the Bible tells me so;
Little ones to Him belong,
They are weak but He is strong.

Anna Bartlett Warner

I have put in my time. I have been on the front lines. I have taught Vacation Bible School. VBS is a wonderful, horrible thing. It's wonderful: getting ready, planning fun activities, making decorations, buying snacks. And it's horrible too: dozens of kiddos to control, weather to worry about, food allergies to consider, discipline to administer, tears to confront. (That last one is the staff.)

For several years I taught VBS. And the same thing happened every year. I started with enthusiasm as a team player. I loved getting ready. I worried about all the little details. The first day was exciting but exhausting. And then by the second day I was over it all, so tired and still four days to go. I loved teaching the kids, but they wore me out. I am the mother of an only child, not prepared for the energy level of a dozen in my charge. YIKES!

At least music time let me rest; finally someone else would be in charge. I took those moments to catch my breath while the kids sang "Deep & Wide," "Father Abraham," and "Jesus Loves Me." You know, baby Christian songs, nothing I needed to listen to.

One year I was having a tough time with my class. They had more energy than I could harness. I plopped down at music time. I let the tunes wash over me. Then I started to really listen to the words. *Little ones to Him belong. They are weak (ha!) but He is strong.* Wait a minute. Jesus loves *me* too. And I am feeling particularly weak. Maybe I should lean on the One who is strong. I didn't get a huge surge of energy, but I got a change in attitude and that helped my VBS week.

Because, you see, every year without fail some kiddo gave me a moment that made it all worthwhile. That moment reminded me why I signed up in the first place. It could be as small as a hug from a very shy camper. Or it could be as big as their dad seeking me out at the week-ending celebration and letting me know how much his camper talks about VBS at home. "You are making an impact. Thanks." But mostly, it was being reminded that Jesus cares for *all* His little ones, including me.

Oh I am weak. Remind me I can lean on Your strength today. You love me!

Amen

So, I command the enjoyment of *Life*

person under the sun than to eat & drink

them in their toil all the days of the

Because There is nothing Better for a & Be Glad. Then joy will accompany Life GOD Has Given Them under The sun.

ecclesiastes 8:15

Acknowledgments

Hooray! I have a book to share! And not just any book, a creation drawn from my heart! Acknowledgments are where you get to use as many exclamations points as you want. And I need a lot of them because I'm excited, and there are so many people to thank! If you've read this far, I can feel you thinking: *Is this going to be one of those very long lists filled with a bunch of names I don't know?* Well yes, and no. Yes because you may not know some of these people, but no because I want to thank you too! So read on.

You are first! Thank you for being a reader willing to color and being an artist willing to read. Thank you for taking the time to relax with me, to play and create and have some fun! I hope you gained all those benefits and more. I really did think of you often as I was working on this book. I hope you have played and prayed!

Now, as you suspected, there are others who really do need to be thanked. And I'm not saving my family for last because they are the best group of in-house cheerleaders I have. My mom, Helen, is my number-one fan. She really is proud of me. She's watched me draw and play and create all my life, and she still gets excited to see what I've been up to. Thanks Mom.

My hubby Rod and son Zach watched me daily create all the work in this book. Zach indulged me every time I needed to bounce around the house and ask, "This is a cool drawing, right?" He'd smile and say, "Yeah it is," with an implied: "And-you'll-make-another-cool-one-tomorrow-and-I'll-be-happy-to-get-excited-about-that-one-too." And Rod always supported me in ways that made me think. He took his time and really looked at what I had done. He found the details to improve. And he was gentle about showing me his thoughts.

There are a few more people who were very important in getting this book into your hands. People like my agent, Janet Grant. She peeked over my shoulder at a conference and said, "You might want to share some of those doodles with your readers." She helped put that suggestion into action with hours of guidance. And then there is my editor, Pamela Clements. She gave me a level of artistic freedom that made me smile daily. The joy to draw anything and the security to know the words would be well tended. And there is Bart Dawson, designer at Worthy. He is the techie to my old school. He made my hand-drawn artwork into something others could color and added his flare to the interior of our book. Janet, Pamela, and Bart were not alone; the whole team at Worthy Inspired Publishing gave hours of crunch time to getting this book to you.

We all sincerely hope you have picked up your colored pencils and markers and enjoyed these pages of our labor of love. Thank you, dear reader, for joining the fun!

About the Author

I went to art school at Colorado State University where I received my Bachelor of Fine Arts degree in 1983. I then worked as a graphic designer for more than a decade before becoming a published author. Design is still an important part of my life. Whether knitting a sweater, remodeling my kitchen, or creating notes to mail to my friends, the aesthetic is always a big part of each project.

I have been doodling since I was a little girl. In fact, some of the images in this book have been perfected over a lifetime. These are pictures I scribble often. And I love lettering. Playing with letter forms is just play for me. And when I can infuse them with meaning, insight or some kind of ah-ha moment for someone else, that's real pleasure.

I recently relocated from San Francisco to Scarsdale, New York, when my husband took a job with HBO. I was excited to be close enough to Manhattan to go in several times a month to take in art and design. Having the Met, the Frick and the Whitney so close is really cool. I love to soak up the sights. Just walking around looking at shop windows, architecture, and people gives me so much inspiration.

I have a part-time job working at Etui Fiber Arts in Larchmont, New York. It's the perfect position for an accomplished knitter. I try not to spend my whole paycheck on more yarn. And it's great to serve other knitters and help them with their projects.

I am also a mom. We have one son. Zachary graduated from Boston University the summer of 2015.

IF YOU ENJOYED THIS BOOK, WILL YOU CONSIDER SHARING THE MESSAGE WITH OTHERS?

Mention the book in a blog post or through Facebook, Twitter, Pinterest, or upload a picture through Instagram.

Recommend this book to those in your small group, book club, workplace, and classes.

Head over to facebook.com/LisaBogartAuthor, "LIKE" the page, and post a comment as to what you enjoyed the most.

Tweet "I recommend reading #DrawnFromTheHeart by Lisa Bogart // @worthypub"

Pick up a copy for someone you know who would be challenged and encouraged by this message.

Write a book review online.

WORTHY®
PUBLISHING

Visit us at worthypublishing.com

twitter.com/worthypub

worthypub.tumblr.com

facebook.com/worthypublishing

pinterest.com/worthypub

instagram.com/worthypub

youtube.com/worthypublishing